GUARD THE HOUSE, SAM!

BY
CHARNAN SIMON

ILLUSTRATED BY
GARY BIALKE

CHILDREN'S PRESS ®
A Division of Grolier Publishing
New York • London • Hong Kong • Sydney
Danbury, Connecticut

For Jill and D. Manus Pinkwater, who have helped
turn many a puppy into a superpuppy
—C. S.

For Bluto, the dog who can drive a car, and the
fine folks at Acme Lint Brush, Inc.
—G. B.

Reading Consultant
Linda Cornwell
Learning Resource Consultant
Indiana Department of Education

Visit Children's Press® on the Internet at:
http://publishing.grolier.com

Library of Congress Cataloging-in-Publication Data

Simon, Charnan.
Guard the house, Sam! / by Charnan Simon ; illustrated by Gary Bialke.
p. cm. — (A rookie reader)
Summary: When Rosie tells her dog to guard the house while she is gone,
he makes a mess everywhere he goes.
ISBN 0-516-20796-2 (lib. bdg.)   0-516-26359-5 (pbk.)
[1. Dogs—Fiction.] I. Bialke, Gary, ill. II. Title. III. Series.
PZ7.S6035Gu 1998
[E] —dc21   97-18796
                                                        CIP
                                                        AC

All rights reserved. Published simultaneously in Canada
Printed in the United States of America
1 2 3 4 5 6 7 8 9 10 R 07 06 05 04 03 02 01 00 99 98

Rosie's dog Sam loved
staying home alone.

"Guard the house, Sam!"
Rosie always said.

Guarding the house was what Sam did best.

First, he looked
downstairs.

9

No burglars there!

11

Next, he looked upstairs.

No burglars there!

14

Sam looked for burglars
in the front yard . . .

17

. . . and in the backyard.

19

DISHES

20

He checked the attic.

He checked the basement.

23

Guarding the kitchen
reminded Sam he was hungry.

Guarding the bathroom reminded Sam he was thirsty.

Guarding the living room reminded Sam he was tired.

29

Guarding the house
was hard work.

ABOUT THE AUTHOR

Charnan Simon has been an editor for *Cricket* magazine and sometimes works at a children's bookstore called Pooh Corner. Mainly, though, she spends her time reading and writing books. Charnan lives in Madison, Wisconsin, with her husband Tom Kazunas, her daughters Ariel and Hana, and the real Sam. This Sam is part collie and part golden retriever, and he is very secretive about what he does when he is home alone. Other Rookie Readers about Sam include *Sam the Garbage Hound* and *Sam and Dasher*.

ABOUT THE ILLUSTRATOR

Gary Bialke's love of shoes, "walkies," and scratching has led him to believe he was a dog in a previous life. Those were good times… sleeping in the sun, eating biscuits, riding in the car, napping, checking for burglars, jumping the fence, napping. Gary still turns around four times before sitting down.